The Tale of Ivarr Son of Ingimundr

Original Text, Translations, and Word Lists

Translated by
Matthew Leigh Embleton

Copyright ©2025 Matthew Leigh Embleton. All rights reserved.

The Tale of Ivarr Son of Ingimundr

The Tale of Ívarr Son of Ingimundr (*Old Norse*) 4
Word List *(Old Norse to English)* 10
Word List *(English to Old Norse)* 16
The Tale of Ívarr Son of Ingimundr (*Old Icelandic*) 21
Word List *(Old Icelandic to English)* 27
Word List *(English to Old Icelandic)* 32
A Word Comparison of Old Norse and Old Icelandic Words 37

Cover: Old Norse text over an outline of Iceland. Author's design.

The original Old Norse and Old Icelandic texts are in the public domain.
These translations ©2022 Matthew Leigh Embleton
©2025 Matthew Leigh Embleton (This Edition)

Acknowledgments

I have long been fascinated by languages and history, and I am very grateful to the special people in my life who have supported and encouraged me in my work. Thank you for believing in me. You know who you are.

Introduction

Old Norse is a North Germanic language spoken by inhabitants of Scandinavia from about the 7th to the 15th centuries. Old Icelandic is a variety of Old West Norse that emerged during the Norse settlement of Iceland in the second half of the 9th century. The rich tradition of Icelandic literature survived by oral tradition over several centuries before being written down in the 13th Century. The Tale of Ívarr Son of Ingimundr (*Ívars þáttr Ingimundarsonar*) is one of the many Tales of Icelanders or *Íslendingaþættir*. The word '*þáttr*' (plural: '*þættir*') translates as a strand of rope or a yarn, comparable to the word 'yarn' in English sometimes used to refer to a story.

This book contains:
- The Tale of Ívarr Son of Ingimundr (Ívars þáttr Ingimundarsonar) (Old Norse Version)
- An Old Norse to English Word List
- An English to Old Norse Word List
- The Tale of Ívarr Son of Ingimundr (Ívars þáttr Ingimundarsonar) (Old Icelandic Version)
- An Old Icelandic to English Word List
- An English to Old Icelandic Word List
- A Word Comparison of Old Norse and Old Icelandic words

The texts are presented in their original form, with a literal word-for-word line-by-line translation, and a Modern English translation, all side-by-side. In this way, it is possible to see and feel how the worked and how it has evolved. This book is designed to be of use and interest to anyone with a passion for the Old Norse or Old Icelandic language, Norse history, or languages and history in general.

The Tale of Ívarr Son of Ingimundr (*Old Norse*)

Old Norse	Literal	English
Í ÞEIMA hlut má marka, er nú mun ek segja, hverr dýrðarmaðr Eysteinn konungr var eða hve mjök hann var vinhollr ok hugkvæmr eftir at leita við sína ástmenn, hvat þeim væri at harmi.	In that part may-be marked, that now shall I say, who glorious-man Eystein king was and how much he was friend-whole and thoughtful after to seek with his beloved-friends, that theirs was of grief.	In part it may be said that I shall now say who the glorious king Eystein was and how much he was a good friend and thoughtful in seeking with his beloved friends what was their grief.
Sá maðr var með Eysteini konungi, er Ívarr hét ok var Ingimundarson, íslenzkr at ætt ok stórættaðr at kyni, vitr maðr ok skáld gott.	That man was with Eystein the-king, was Ivar named and was Son-of-Ingimundur, Icelander by ancestry and large-family to kin, wise man and poet good.	That man was with Eystein the king and was named Ivar and he was the son of Ingimundur, an Icelander by ancestry with a large family and kin, a wise man and a good poet.
Konungr virði hann mikils ok var til hans ástsamliga, sem sýnist í þessum hlut.	The-king worthed him much and was to him affectionate, as seems in this matter.	The king valued him very much and was affectionate to him as it seems in this matter.
Þorfinnr hét bróðir Ívars.	Thorfin was-named brother Ivar's.	Ivar's brother was named Thorfin.
Hann fór ok útan á fund Eysteins konungs ok naut þar mjök frá [mörgum mönnum] bróður síns.	He travelled and out to meet Eystein the-king and enjoyed there much from [many men] brother his.	He travelled out to meet Eystein the king and enjoyed much of his brother's popularity with many men there.
En honum þótti þat mikit, er hann skyldi eigi þykkja jafnmenni bróður síns ok þurfa hans at njóta, ok unði af því eigi með konungi ok bjóst út til Íslands.	But he thought it much, that he should not be-valued equal-to brother his and needed he to enjoy, and part off therefore not with the-king and prepare out to Iceland.	But he thought it was a bit much that he was not valued as equal to his brother, on whom he depended for that which he enjoyed, and therefore parted with the king and prepared to travel out to Iceland.
Ok áðr en þeir bræðr skildist, mælti Ívarr, at Þorfiðr skyldi þau orð bera Oddnýju Jóansdóttur, at hon biði hans ok giftist eigi, lét sér um hana mest vera allra kvenna.	And before that they brothers parted, said Ivar, that Thorfin should then word carry Oddynja Joansdottir, that she wait-for him and be-married not, had he about her the-most being of-all women.	And before the brothers parted Ivar said that Thorfin should carry word to Oddynja Joansdottir for her to wait for him and not marry, for he held her above all other women.
Síðan ferr Þorfinnr út ok varð vel reiðfari ok tók þat ráð, at hann bað Oddnýjar sér til handa ok fekk hennar.	Then travelled Thorfin out and was well travelled and took the decision, that he ask Oddny her to hand and married her.	Then Thorfin fared out and travelled well, and he decided to ask Oddyn for her hand in marriage himself.

The Tale of Ívarr Son of Ingimundr (Old Norse)

Old Norse	Literal	English
Ok litlu síðar kom Ívarr út ok frá þetta ok þótti Þorfiðr illa hafa ór haft við sik, ok unir hann engu ok ferr aftr síðan til konungs ok er með honum í góðu yfirlæti sem fyrr.	And a-little later came Ivar out and of this and thought Thorfin bad having of had with him, and satisfied he-was none and travelled back afterwards to the-king and was with him in good favour as before.	And a little later Ivar came out to Iceland and heard about this, and thought that Thorfin had done bad to him, and he was most unsatisfied, and travelled back to the king and was held in good favour with him as before.
Ívarr tekr nú ógleði mikla, ok er konungr fann þat, heimtí hann Ívar til máls við sik ok spurði, hví hann væri svá ókátr, - "ok fyrr, er þér váruð með oss, var margs konar skemmtan at yðrum orðum,	Ivar took now sadness much, and as the-king found it, summoned he Ivar to speak with him and asked, why he was so displeased, "and before, when you were with us, were many kinds-of amusement from your words,	Ivar took to a great sadness and when the king noticed he summoned Ivar to speak with him and asked him why he was so displeased "Whereas before when you were with us, there was much amusement from your words.
ok eigi leita ek fyrir því eftir þessu, at eigi vita ek, at vér höfum ekki af gert við þik.	and not asking I for since after this, that not knew I, that we have not of done with you.	And I do not ask since we do know know if it is because we have wronged you.
Ertu ok svá vitr maðr, at eigi muntu grun draga af því, er eigi er, ok seg mér, hvat er".	You-are and such wise man, that not should-you suspicion drag of therefore, if not is, and say to-me, what is".	For you are such a wise man that you would not suspect a slight where none exists, and please tell me what it is".
Ívarr svaraði:	Ivar answered:	Ivar answered:
"Þat, sem er, herra, má ek ekki frá segja".	"That, which is, lord, may I not from say".	"What it is lord I may not say".
Konungr mælti:	The-King said:	The king said:
"Ek mun þá geta til.	"I should then guess to.	"Then I should gess it.
Eru nökkurir menn, þeir er þér getist eigi at?"	Is-there some man, they who to-you estimate not of?"	Is there some man who you do not hold in esteem?"
"Eigi er þat, herra", segir Ívarr.	"Not is that, lord", said Ivar.	"It is not that, lord", said Ivar.
Konungr mælti:	The-King said:	The king said:
"Þykkist þú af mér hafa minna sóma en þú vildir?"	"Seeming to-you of me have less honour that you wish?"	"Do you think of me that I have less honour than you wish?".
"Eigi er þat, herra", segir hann.	"Not is that, lord", said he.	"It is not that, lord", said he.

The Tale of Ívarr Son of Ingimundr (Old Norse)

Old Norse	Literal	English
"Hefir þú sét nökkura hluti", segir konungr, "þá er þér hafa svá mikit um fundizt hér í landinu?"	"Have you seen any things", said the-king, "then that to-you have so greatly about found here in the-land?"	"Have you seen anything", said the king, "that you have found in this land which you covet?".
Hann kveðr eigi þat vera.	He said not that was.	He said that it was not that.
"Vandast oss nú getan", segir konungr.	"Difficult ours now guessing", said the-king.	"It is now difficult for us to guess", said the king.
"Villtu hafa forræði nökkur yfir eignum nökkurum?"	"Will-you to-have power any over owning anything?"	"Do you wish to have authority over or some ownership of something?".
Hann neitti því.	He nothing such.	He said it was nothing as such.
"Eru nökkurar konur þær á yðru landi", segir konungr, "er þér sé eftirsjá at?"	"Are-there some woman therefore that your land", said the-king, "that you yourself look-back to?"	"Are there any women there in your land", said the king, "that you look back to with regret?".
Hann svaraði:	He answered:	He answered:
"Svá er, herra".	"So it-is, lord".	"So it is, lord".
Konungr mælti:	The-King said:	The king said:
"Ver eigi þar um hugsjúkr.	"Be not therefore about-it mind-sick.	"Therefore do not be anxious about it.
Þegar er várar, far þú út.	As-soon as spring, travel you out.	As soon as the spring comes you shall travel out.
Mun ek fá þér fé ok bréf mitt með innsigli til þeira manna, er ráða eigu, ok veit ek eigi þeira manna vánir, at eigi víkja eftir várum vinmælum eða ógnarorðum at gifta konuna".	Shall I give you wealth and letters mine with royal-seal to those men, who power posess, and know I not they people's hopes, that not give-in after our friendly-words or menacing-words to give-in-marriage this-woman".	I shall give you wealth and letters with a royal seal to those men who have the authority, and I do not know of anyone who will not give in after our friendly words or menacing words to give this woman in marriage".
Ívarr svaraði:	Ivar answered:	Ivar answered:
"Eigi má svá vera".	"Not may so be".	"It may not be so".
Konungr mælti:	The-King said:	The king said:

The Tale of Ívarr Son of Ingimundr (Old Norse)

Old Norse	Literal	English
"Engi veg má þess vera", segir konungr.	"No way may this be", said the-king.	"There is no way this may be", said the king.
"Því mun ek mæla framar, þó at annarr maðr eigi hana, þá mun ek þó ná, ef ek vil, þér til handa".	"Therefore shall I say from, yet that another man owns her, then shall I nevertheless get, if I wish, you to hand".	"Therefore I shall say that yet another man owns her, then I shall nevertheless get her if you wish for her hand".
Ívarr svaraði:	Ivar answered:	Ivar answered:
"Þungligar er farit málinu, herra.	"Is going the-matter lord, lord.	"This is where the matter becomes difficult, lord.
Bróðir minn á nú konuna".	Brother mine has now a-wife".	My brother now has her as a wife".
Þá mælti konungr:	Then said the-king:	Then the king said:
"Hverfum þar frá", segir hann.	"Let-us-go here from", said he.	"Then let us go from here", he said.
"Sé ek þá ráð til.	"Say I then advise to.	"I say then to advise.
Eftir jólin mun ek fara á veizlur, ok far þú með mér, ok muntu þar sjá margar kurteisar konur, ok ef eigi eru konungbornar, þá mun ek fá þér einhverja".	After Yule shall I travel to feasts, and travel you with me, and shall there see many polite women, and if none are kings-born, then shall I get you one".	After Yule I shall travel to feasts and you shall travel with me and you shall see there many polite women, and if there are no kings born, then I shall get you one".
Ívarr svaraði:	Ivar answered:	Ivar answered:
"Herra, því þungligar er komit mínu máli, at jafnan, er ek sé fagrar konur, þá minnir mik þessar konu, ok er æ því meiri minn harmr".	"Lord, because the-heavier has become my matter, to equally, that I see fair woman, then memory mine this woman, and is ever therefore greater my grief".	"Lord, because my matter has become heavier, equally when I see a fair woman then I have memory of this woman, and my grief is ever therefore greater".
Konungr mælti:	The-King said:	The king said:
"Þá mun ek gefa þér nökkur forræði ok eigur, sem ek bauð þér fyrr, ok skemmtir þú þér við þat".	"Then shall I give to-you some authority and ownership, which I offered you before, and amuse you yourself with that".	"Then I shall give to you some authority and ownership which I offered you before and you can amuse yourself with that".
Hann svaraði:	He answered:	He answered:

The Tale of Ívarr Son of Ingimundr (Old Norse)

Old Norse	Literal	English
"Ekki uni ek því".	"Not like I that".	"I do not like that".
Konungr mælti:	The-King said:	The king said:
"Þá fæ ek þér lausafé, ok ferr þú kaupferðir þangat til landa, sem þú vill".	"Then give I to-you free-wealth, and travel you shopping-travelling there to lands, as you wish".	"Then I give to you free wealth and you may travel and purchase there lands as you wish".
Hann lézt eigi þat vildu.	He had not that willed.	He said that he did not wish for this.
Þá mælti konungr:	Then said the-king:	Then the king said:
"Vandast mér nú heldr, því at eftir hefi ek nú leitat sem ek kann.	"Difficult for-me now rather, because that after have I now sought that-which I can.	"This is rather difficult for me now after I have sought all that I can.
Ok er nú einn eftir hlutrinn, ok er sá alllítils verðr hjá þessum, er ek hefi boðit þér, en þó kann eigi geta, hvat helzt hlýðir.	And is it now one after thing, and is so little worth next-to these, that I have offered to-you, but though know not get, what preferably obeys.	And now there is one thing after that is of little worth next to these that I have offered to you, but though one can not know what is best".
Far þú nú hvern dag, þá er borð eru uppi, á fund minn, ok ek sitk eigi um nauðsynjamálum, ok mun ek hjala við þik.	Travel you now each day, then to tables they-are up, to find mine, and I sit not about needful-matters, and shall I talk with you.	"You shall travel each day then to my tables when they are up to find me, when I am not sitting on needful matters, and I shall talk with you.
Skulum vit ræða um konu þessa alla vega, þess er þú [vill] ok má í hug koma, ok mun ek gefa mér tóm til þessa, því at þat verðr stundum, at mönnum verðr harms síns at léttara, er um er rætt.	We-shall with discuss about woman this all ways, this that you wish and may to thought come, and shall I give myself time to this, accordingly that it becomes awhile, that men becomes sorrow theirs that lightened, are about is discussed.	We-shall with discuss about this woman all ways that you wish and may come to mind, and shall I give myself time to this accordingly, that it becomes after a while that men's sorrow becomes lightened when it is talked about.
Ok þat skal ok þessu fylgja, at aldri skaltu gjaflaust í brott fara frá mínum fundi".	And that shall and this follow, that never shall-you giftless to away travel from my meeting".	And this shall follow, that you shall never travel away from my meeting without a gift".
Ívarr svaraði:	Ivar answered:	Ivar answered:
"Þetta vil ek, herra, ok haf þökk fyrir eftirleitunina".	"That will I, lord, and have thanks for after-seeking".	"That I wish for lord, and I have thanks for your consideration".

The Tale of Ívarr Son of Ingimundr (Old Norse)

Old Norse	Literal	English
Ok nú gera þeir svá, at jafnan, er konungr sitr eigi yfir vandamálum, þá talar hann oft um þessa konu við Ívar.	And now did they so, to equally, and the-king sat not over problems, then talk he often about this woman with Ivar.	And now they did so, equally the king sat over problems, and then talked often about this woman with Ivar.
Ok þetta hlýddi bragðit, ok bættist nú Ívari harms síns vánum bráðara.	And this followed looked, and improved now Ivar's grief his hoped sooner-than.	And so it followed, that it looked that now to Ivar that his grief improved sonner than he had hoped.
Gladdist hann eftir þetta, ok kemr í samt lag sem fyrr hafði verit um skemmtun hans ok gleði.	Gladdest he after this, and came to same place as before had been about amusement his and gladness.	Gladdened was he after this, and it came to the same as it was before, his amusement and gladness.
Ok er hann með Eysteini.	And was he with Eystein.	And he remained with Eystein.

Word List *(Old Norse to English)*

Old Norse	English

A, a

af	of, off
aftr	back
aldri	never
alla	all
alllítils	little
allra	of-all
annarr	another
at	by, from, of, that, to

Á, á

á	has, that, to
áðr	before
ástmenn	beloved-friends
ástsamliga	affectionate

Æ, æ

æ	ever
ætt	ancestry

B, b

bað	ask
bættist	improved
bauð	offered
bera	carry
biði	wait-for
bjóst	prepare
boðit	offered
borð	tables
bráðara	sooner-than
bræðr	brothers
bragðit	looked
bréf	letters
bróðir	brother
bróður	brother
brott	away

D, d

dag	day
draga	drag
dýrðarmaðr	glorious-man

E, e

eða	and, or
ef	if
eftir	after
eftirleitunina	after-seeking
eftirsjá	look-back
eigi	none, not, owns
eignum	owning
eigu	posess
eigur	ownership
einhverja	one
einn	one
ek	I
ekki	not
en	but, that
engi	no
engu	none
er	and, are, as, going, has, if, is, is it, it-is, that, to, was, when, who
ertu	you-are
eru	are, are-there, is-there, they-are
Eysteini	Eystein (name)
Eysteinn	Eystein (name)
Eysteins	Eystein (name)

F, f

fá	get, give
fæ	give

Word List (Old Norse to English)

Old Norse	English
fagrar	fair
fann	found
far	travel
fara	travel
farit	the-matter
fé	wealth
fekk	married
ferr	travel, travelled
fór	travelled
forræði	authority, power
frá	from, of
framar	from
fund	find, meet
fundi	meeting
fundizt	found
fylgja	follow
fyrir	for
fyrr	before

G, g

Old Norse	English
gefa	give
gera	did
gert	done
geta	get, guess
getan	guessing
getist	estimate
gifta	give-in-marriage
giftist	be-married
gjaflaust	gitfless
gladdist	gladdest
gleði	gladness
góðu	good
gott	good
grun	suspicion

H, h

Old Norse	English
haf	have
hafa	have, having, to-have
hafði	had
haft	had
hana	her
handa	hand
hann	he, he-was, him
hans	he, him, his
harmi	grief
harmr	grief
harms	grief, sorrow
hefi	have
hefir	have
heimtí	summoned
heldr	rather
helzt	preferably
hennar	her
hér	here
herra	lord
hét	named, was-named
hjá	next-to
hjala	talk
hlut	matter, part
hluti	things
hlutrinn	thing
hlýddi	followed
hlýðir	obeys
höfum	have
hon	she
honum	he, him
hug	thought
hugkvæmr	thoughtful
hugsjúkr	mind-sick
hvat	that, what
hve	how
hverfum	let-us-go
hvern	each
hverr	who
hví	why

I, i

Old Norse	English
illa	bad
Ingimundarson	son-of-Ingimundur (name)
innsigli	royal-seal

Word List (Old Norse to English)

Old Norse	English

Í, í

Old Norse	English
í	in, to
Íslands	Iceland (place)
íslenzkr	Icelander
Ívar	Ivar (name)
Ívari	Ivar's (name)
Ívarr	Ivar (name)
Ívars	Ivar's (name)

J, j

Old Norse	English
jafnan	equally
jafnmenni	equal-to
Jóansdóttur	Joansdottir (name)
jólin	Yule

K, k

Old Norse	English
kann	can, know
kaupferðir	shopping-travelling
kemr	came
kom	came
koma	come
komit	become
konar	kinds-of
konu	woman
konuna	a-wife, this-woman
konungbornar	kings-born
konungi	the-king
konungr	king, the-king
konungs	the-king
konur	woman, women
kurteisar	polite
kveðr	said
kvenna	women
kyni	kin

L, l

Old Norse	English
lag	place
landa	lands
landi	land
landinu	the-land
lausafé	free-wealth
leita	asking, seek
leitat	sought
lét	had
léttara	lightened
lézt	had
litlu	a-little

M, m

Old Norse	English
má	may, may-be
maðr	man
mæla	say
mælti	said
máli	matter
málinu	lord
máls	speak
manna	men, people's
margar	many
margs	many
marka	marked
með	with
meiri	greater
menn	man
mér	for-me, me, myself, to-me
mest	the-most
mik	mine
mikils	much
mikit	greatly, much
mikla	much
minn	mine, my
minna	less
minnir	memory
mínu	my
minum	my
mitt	mine
mjök	much
mönnum	men
mörgum	many
mun	shall, should
muntu	shall, should-you

Word List (Old Norse to English)

Old Norse	English
N, n	
ná	get
nauðsynjamálum	needful-matters
naut	enjoyed
neitti	nothing
njóta	enjoy
nökkur	any, some
nökkura	any
nökkurar	some
nökkurir	some
nökkurum	anything
nú	now
O, o	
Oddnýjar	Oddny (name)
Oddnýju	Oddynja (name)
oft	often
ok	and
orð	word
orðum	words
oss	ours, us
Ó, ó	
ógleði	sadness
ógnarorðum	menacing-words
ókátr	displeased
ór	of
R, r	
ráð	advise, decision
ráða	power
ræða	discuss
rætt	discussed
reiðfari	travelled
S, s	
sá	so, that
samt	same
sé	say, see, yourself
seg	say
segir	said
segja	say
sem	as, that-which, which
sér	he, her
sét	seen
síðan	afterwards, then
síðar	later
sik	him
sína	his
síns	his, theirs
sitk	sit
sitr	sat
sjá	see
skal	shall
skáld	poet
skaltu	shall-you
skemmtan	amusement
skemmtir	amuse
skemmtun	amusement
skilðist	parted
skulum	we-shall
skyldi	should
sóma	honour
spurði	asked
stórættaðr	large-family
stundum	awhile
svá	so, such
svaraði	answered
sýnist	seems
T, t	
talar	talk
tekr	took
til	to
tók	took
tóm	time

Word List (Old Norse to English)

Old Norse	English
Þ, þ	
þá	then
þær	therefore
þangat	there
þar	here, there, there, therefore
þat	it, that, the
þau	then
þegar	as-soon
þeim	theirs
þeima	that
þeir	they
þeira	they, those
þér	to-you, you, yourself
þess	this
þessa	this
þessar	this
þessu	this
þessum	these, this
þetta	that, this
þik	you
þó	nevertheless, though, yet
þökk	thanks
Þorfiðr	Thorfin (name), Thorfin (name)
Þorfinnr	Thorfin (name), Thorfin (name)
þótti	thought, thought
þú	to-you, you
þungligar	is, the-heavier
þurfa	needed
því	accordingly, because, since, such, that, therefore
þykkist	seeming
þykkja	be-valued
U, u	
um	about, about-it
unði	part
uni	like
unir	satisfied
uppi	up
Ú, ú	
út	out
útan	out
V, v	
væri	was
vandamálum	problems
vandast	difficult
vánir	hopes
vánum	hoped
var	was, were
várar	spring
varð	was
váruð	were
várum	our
veg	way
vega	ways
veit	know
veizlur	feasts
vel	well
ver	be
vér	we
vera	be, being, was
verðr	becomes, worth
verit	been
við	with
víkja	give-in
vil	will, wish
vildir	wish
vildu	willed
vill	wish
villtu	will-you
vinhollr	friend-whole
vinmælum	friendly-words
virði	worthed
vit	with
vita	knew
vitr	wise

Word List (Old Norse to English)

Old Norse   English

Y, y

yðru	your
yðrum	your
yfir	over
yfirlæti	favour

# Word List *(English to Old Norse)*

English	Old Norse
A, a	
about	um
about-it	um
accordingly	því
advise	ráð
affectionate	ástsamliga
after	eftir
after-seeking	eftirleitunina
afterwards	síðan
a-little	litlu
all	alla
amuse	skemmtir
amusement	skemmtan, skemmtun
ancestry	ætt
and	eða, er, ok
another	annarr
answered	svaraði
any	nökkur, nökkura
anything	nökkurum
are	er, eru
are-there	eru
as	er, sem
ask	bað
asked	spurði
asking	leita
as-soon	þegar
authority	forræði
away	brott
awhile	stundum
a-wife	konuna
B, b	
back	aftr
bad	illa
be	ver, vera
because	því
become	komit
becomes	verðr
been	verit
before	áðr, fyrr
being	vera
beloved-friends	ástmenn
be-married	giftist
be-valued	þykkja
brother	bróðir, bróður
brothers	bræðr
but	en
by	at
C, c	
came	kemr, kom
can	kann
carry	bera
come	koma
D, d	
day	dag
decision	ráð
did	gera
difficult	vandast
discuss	ræða
discussed	rætt
displeased	ókátr
done	gert
drag	draga
E, e	
each	hvern
enjoy	njóta
enjoyed	naut
equally	jafnan
equal-to	jafnmenni
estimate	getist
ever	æ
Eystein (name)	Eysteini, Eysteinn, Eysteins

Word List (English to Old Norse)

English	Old Norse

F, f

fair	fagrar
favour	yfirlæti
feasts	veizlur
find	fund
follow	fylgja
followed	hlýddi
for	fyrir
for-me	mér
found	fann, fundizt
free-wealth	lausafé
friendly-words	vinmælum
friend-whole	vinhollr
from	at, frá, framar

G, g

get	fá, geta, ná
gitfless	gjaflaust
give	fá, fæ, gefa
give-in	víkja
give-in-marriage	gifta
gladdest	gladdist
gladness	gleði
glorious-man	dýrðarmaðr
going	er
good	góðu, gott
greater	meiri
greatly	mikit
grief	harmi, harmr, harms
guess	geta
guessing	getan

H, h

had	hafði, haft, lét, lézt
hand	handa
has	á, er
have	haf, hafa, hefi, hefir, höfum
having	hafa

English	Old Norse

he	hann, hans, honum, sér
her	hana, hennar, sér
here	hér, þar
he-was	hann
him	hann, hans, honum, sik
his	hans, sína, síns
honour	sóma
hoped	vánum
hopes	vánir
how	hve

I, i

I	ek
Iceland (place)	Íslands
Icelander	íslenzkr
if	ef, er
improved	bættist
in	í
is	er, þungligar
is it	er
is-there	eru
it	þat
it-is	er
Ivar (name)	Ívar, Ívarr
Ivar's (name)	Ívari, Ívars

J, j

Joansdottir (name)	Jóansdóttur

K, k

kin	kyni
kinds-of	konar
king	konungr
kings-born	konungbornar
knew	vita
know	kann, veit

Word List (English to Old Norse)

English	Old Norse

L, l

land	landi
lands	landa
large-family	stórættaðr
later	síðar
less	minna
letters	bréf
let-us-go	hverfum
lightened	léttara
like	uni
little	alllítils
look-back	eftirsjá
looked	bragðit
lord	herra, málinu

M, m

man	maðr, menn
many	margar, margs, mörgum
marked	marka
married	fekk
matter	hlut, máli
may	má
may-be	má
me	mér
meet	fund
meeting	fundi
memory	minnir
men	manna, mönnum
menacing-words	ógnarorðum
mind-sick	hugsjúkr
mine	mik, minn, mitt
much	mikils, mikit, mikla, mjök
my	minn, mínu, minum
myself	mér

N, n

named	hét
needed	þurfa

English	Old Norse
needful-matters	nauðsynjamálum
never	aldri
nevertheless	þó
next-to	hjá
no	engi
none	eigi, engu
not	eigi, ekki
nothing	neitti
now	nú

O, o

obeys	hlýðir
Oddny (name)	Oddnýjar
Oddynja (name)	Oddnýju
of	af, at, frá, ór
of-all	allra
off	af
offered	bauð, boðit
often	oft
one	einhverja, einn
or	eða
our	várum
ours	oss
out	út, útan
over	yfir
ownership	eigur
owning	eignum
owns	eigi

P, p

part	hlut, unði
parted	skilðist
people's	manna
place	lag
poet	skáld
polite	kurteisar
posess	eigu
power	forræði, ráða
preferably	helzt
prepare	bjóst
problems	vandamálum

Word List (English to Old Norse)

English	Old Norse
R, r	
rather	heldr
royal-seal	innsigli
S, s	
sadness	ógleði
said	kveðr, mælti, segir
same	samt
sat	sitr
satisfied	unir
say	mæla, sé, seg, segja
see	sé, sjá
seek	leita
seeming	þykkist
seems	sýnist
seen	sét
shall	mun, muntu, skal
shall-you	skaltu
she	hon
shopping-travelling	kaupferðir
should	mun, skyldi
should-you	muntu
since	því
sit	sitk
so	sá, svá
some	nökkur, nökkurar, nökkurir
son-of-Ingimundur (name)	Ingimundarson
sooner-than	bráðara
sorrow	harms
sought	leitat
speak	máls
spring	várar
such	svá, því
summoned	heimtí
suspicion	grun
T, t	
tables	borð

English	Old Norse
talk	hjala, talar
thanks	þökk
that	á, at, en, er, hvat, sá, þat, þeima, þetta, því
that-which	sem
the	þat
the-heavier	þungligar
theirs	síns, þeim
the-king	konungi, konungr, konungs
the-land	landinu
the-matter	farit
the-most	mest
then	síðan, þá, þau
there	þangat, þar, þar
therefore	þær, þar, því
these	þessum
they	þeir, þeira
they-are	eru
thing	hlutrinn
things	hluti
this	þess, þessa, þessar, þessu, þessum, þetta
this-woman	konuna
Thorfin (name)	Þorfiðr, Þorfiðr, Þorfinnr, Þorfinnr
those	þeira
though	þó
thought	hug, þótti, þótti
thoughtful	hugkvæmr
time	tóm
to	á, at, er, í, til
to-have	hafa
to-me	mér
took	tekr, tók
to-you	þér, þú
travel	far, fara, ferr
travelled	ferr, fór, reiðfari
U, u	
up	uppi
us	oss

Word List (English to Old Norse)

English Old Norse

W, w

wait-for	biði
was	er, væri, var, varð, vera
was-named	hét
way	veg
ways	vega
we	vér
wealth	fé
well	vel
were	var, váruð
we-shall	skulum
what	hvat
when	er
which	sem
who	er, hverr
why	hví
will	vil
willed	vildu
will-you	villtu
wise	vitr
wish	vil, vildir, vill
with	með, við, vit
woman	konu, konur
women	konur, kvenna
word	orð
words	orðum
worth	verðr
worthed	virði

Y, y

yet	þó
you	þér, þik, þú
you-are	ertu
your	yðru, yðrum
yourself	sé, þér
Yule	jólin

The Tale of Ívarr Son of Ingimundr (*Old Icelandic*)

Old Icelandic	Literal	English
Í þeima hlut má marka er nú mun eg segja hver dýrðarmaður Eysteinn konungur var eða hve mjög hann var vinhollur og hugkvæmur eftir að leita við sína ástmenn hvað þeim væri að harmi.	In that part may-be marked that now shall I say who glorious-man Eystein king was and how much he was friend-whole and thoughtful after to seek with his beloved-friends that theirs was of grief.	In part it may be said that I shall now say who the glorious king Eystein was and how much he was a good friend and thoughtful in seeking with his beloved friends what was their grief.
Sá maður var með Eysteini konungi er Ívar hét og var Ingimundarson, íslenskur að ætt og stórættaður að kyni, vitur maður og skáld gott.	That man was with Eystein the-king was Ivar named and was Son-of-Ingimundur, Icelander by ancestry and large-family to kin, wise man and poet good.	That man was with Eystein the king and was named Ivar and he was the son of Ingimundur, an Icelander by ancestry with a large family and kin, a wise man and a good poet.
Konungur virti hann mikils og var til hans ástsamlega sem sýnist í þessum hlut.	The-king worthed him much and was to him affectionate as seems in this matter.	The king valued him very much and was affectionate to him as it seems in this matter.
Þorfinnur hét bróðir Ívars.	Thorfin was-named brother Ivar's.	Ivar's brother was named Thorfin.
Hann fór og utan á fund Eysteins konungs og naut þar mjög frá mörgum mönnum bróður síns.	He travelled and out to meet Eystein the-king and enjoyed there much from many men brother his.	He travelled out to meet Eystein the king and enjoyed much of his brother's popularity with many men there.
En honum þótti það mikið er hann skyldi eigi þykja jafnmenni bróður síns og þurfa hans að njóta og undi af því eigi með konungi og bjóst út til Íslands.	But he thought it much that he should not be-valued equal-to brother his and needed he to enjoy and part off therefore not with the-king and prepare out to Iceland.	But he thought it was a bit much that he was not valued as equal to his brother, on whom he depended for that which he enjoyed, and therefore parted with the king and prepared to travel out to Iceland.
Og áður en þeir bræður skildust mælti Ívar að Þorfinnur skyldi þau orð bera Oddnýju Jóansdóttur að hún biði hans og giftist eigi, lét sér um hana mest vera allra kvenna.	And before that they brothers parted said Ivar that Thorfin should then word carry Oddynja Joansdottir that she wait-for him and be-married not, had he about her the-most being of-all women.	And before the brothers parted Ivar said that Thorfin should carry word to Oddynja Joansdottir for her to wait for him and not marry, for he held her above all other women.
Síðan fer Þorfinnur út og varð vel reiðfari og tók það ráð að hann bað Oddnýjar sér til handa og fékk hennar.	Then travelled Thorfin out and was well travelled and took the decision that he ask Oddny her to hand and married her.	Then Thorfin fared out and travelled well, and he decided to ask Oddyn for her hand in marriage himself.

The Tale of Ívarr Son of Ingimundr (Old Icelandic)

Old Icelandic	Literal	English
Og litlu síðar kom Ívar út og frá þetta og þótti Þorfinnur illa hafa úr haft við sig og unir hann öngu og fer aftur síðan til konungs og er með honum í góðu yfirlæti sem fyrr.	And a-little later came Ivar out and of this and thought Thorfin bad having of had with him and satisfied he-was none and travelled back afterwards to the-king and was with him in good favour as before.	And a little later Ivar came out to Iceland and heard about this, and thought that Thorfin had done bad to him, and he was most unsatisfied, and travelled back to the king and was held in good favour with him as before.
Ívar tekur nú ógleði mikla og er konungur fann það heimti hann Ívar til máls við sig og spurði hví hann væri svo ókátur og fyrr er þér voruð með oss var margs konar skemmtan að yðrum orðum.	Ivar took now sadness much and as the-king found it summoned he Ivar to speak with him and asked why he was so displeased and before when you were with us were many kinds-of amusement from your words.	Ivar took to a great sadness and when the king noticed he summoned Ivar to speak with him and asked him why he was so displeased "Whereas before when you were with us, there was much amusement from your words.
Og eigi leita eg fyrir því eftir þessu að eigi viti eg að vér höfum ekki af gert við þig.	And not asking I for since after this that not knew I that we have not of done with you.	And I do not ask since we do know know if it is because we have wronged you.
Ertu og svo vitur maður að eigi muntu grun draga af því er eigi er og seg mér hvað er.	You-are and such wise man that not should-you suspicion drag of therefore if not is and say to-me what is.	For you are such a wise man that you would not suspect a slight where none exists, and please tell me what it is".
Ívar svaraði:	Ivar answered:	Ivar answered:
"Það sem er herra má eg ekki frá segja.	"That which is lord may I not from say".	"What it is lord I may not say".
Konungur mælti:	The-King said:	The king said:
"Eg mun þá geta til.	"I should then guess to	"Then I should gess it.
Eru nokkurir menn þeir er þér getist eigi að?	Is-there some man they who to-you estimate not of?"	Is there some man who you do not hold in esteem?"
Eigi er það herra, segir Ívar.	Not is that lord, said Ivar.	"It is not that, lord", said Ivar.
Konungur mælti:	The-King said:	The king said:
"Þykist þú af mér hafa minna sóma en þú vildir?	"Seeming to-you of me have less honour that you wish?"	"Do you think of me that I have less honour than you wish?".
"Eigi er það herra, segir hann.	"Not is that lord, said he.	"It is not that, lord", said he.

The Tale of Ívarr Son of Ingimundr (Old Icelandic)

Old Icelandic	Literal	English
"Hefir þú séð nokkura hluti, segir konungur, "þá er þér hafa svo mikið um fundist hér í landinu?	"Have you seen any things, said the-king, "then that to-you have so greatly about found here in the-land?"	"Have you seen anything", said the king, "that you have found in this land which you covet?".
Hann kveður eigi það vera.	He said not that was.	He said that it was not that.
"Vandast oss nú getan, segir konungur.	"Difficult ours now guessing, said the-king.	"It is now difficult for us to guess", said the king.
"Viltu hafa forræði nokkur yfir eignum nokkurum?	"Will-you to-have power any over owning anything?"	"Do you wish to have authority over or some ownership of something?".
Hann neitti því.	He nothing such.	He said it was nothing as such.
"Eru nokkurar konur þær á yðru landi, segir konungur, "er þér sé eftirsjá að?	"Are-there some woman therefore that your land" said the-king, "that you yourself look-back to?"	"Are there any women there in your land", said the king, "that you look back to with regret?".
Hann svaraði:	He answered:	He answered:
"Svo er herra.	"So it-is lord".	"So it is, lord".
Konungur mælti:	The-King said:	The king said:
"Ver eigi þar um hugsjúkur.	"Be not therefore about-it mind-sick.	"Therefore do not be anxious about it.
Þegar er vorar far þú út.	As-soon as spring travel you out.	As soon as the spring comes you shall travel out.
Mun eg fá þér fé og bréf mitt með innsigli til þeirra manna er ráða eiga og veit eg eigi þeirra manna vonir að eigi víkja eftir vorum vinmælum eða ógnarorðum að gifta konuna.	Shall I give you wealth and letters mine with royal-seal to those men who power posess and know I not they people's hopes that not give-in after our friendly-words or menacing-words to give-in-marriage this-woman".	I shall give you wealth and letters with a royal seal to those men who have the authority, and I do not know of anyone who will not give in after our friendly words or menacing words to give this woman in marriage".
Ívar svaraði:	Ivar answered:	Ivar answered:
"Eigi má svo vera.	"Not may so be".	"It may not be so".
Konungur mælti:	The-King said:	The king said:

The Tale of Ívarr Son of Ingimundr (Old Icelandic)

Old Icelandic	Literal	English
"Engi veg má þess vera, segir konungur.	"No way may this be, said the-king.	"There is no way this may be", said the king.
"Því mun eg mæla framar þó að annar maður eigi hana þá mun eg þó ná ef eg vil þér til handa.	"Therefore shall I say from yet that another man owns her then shall I nevertheless get if I wish you to hand".	"Therefore I shall say that yet another man owns her, then I shall nevertheless get her if you wish for her hand".
Ívar svaraði:	Ivar answered:	Ivar answered:
"Þunglegar er farið málinu herra.	"Difficult is going the-matter lord.	"This is where the matter becomes difficult, lord.
Bróðir minn á nú konuna.	Brother mine has now a-wife".	My brother now has her as a wife".
Þá mælti konungur:	Then said the-king:	Then the king said:
"Hverfum þar frá, segir hann.	"Let-us-go here from, said he.	"Then let us go from here", he said.
"Sé eg þá ráð til.	"Say I then advise to.	"I say then to advise.
Eftir jólin mun eg fara á veislur og far þú með mér og muntu þar sjá margar kurteisar konur og ef eigi eru konungbornar þá mun eg fá þér einhverja.	After Yule shall I travel to feasts and travel you with me and shall there see many polite women and if none are kings-born then shall I get you one".	After Yule I shall travel to feasts and you shall travel with me and you shall see there many polite women, and if there are no kings born, then I shall get you one".
Ívar svaraði:	Ivar answered:	Ivar answered:
"Herra, því þunglegar er komið mínu máli að jafnan er eg sé fagrar konur þá minnir mig þessar konu og er æ því meiri minn harmur.	"Lord, because the-heavier has become my matter to equally that I see fair woman then memory mine this woman and is ever therefore greater my grief"	"Lord, because my matter has become heavier, equally when I see a fair woman then I have memory of this woman, and my grief is ever therefore greater".
Konungur mælti:	The-King said:	The king said:
"Þá mun eg gefa þér nokkur forræði og eigur sem eg bauð þér fyrr og skemmtir þú þér við það.	"Then shall I give to-you some authority and ownership which I offered you before and amuse you yourself with that".	"Then I shall give to you some authority and ownership which I offered you before and you can amuse yourself with that".
Hann svaraði:	He answered:	He answered:

The Tale of Ívarr Son of Ingimundr (Old Icelandic)

Old Icelandic	Literal	English
"Ekki uni eg því.	"Not like I that".	"I do not like that".
Konungur mælti:	The-King said:	The king said:
"Þá fæ eg þér lausafé og ferð þú kaupferðir þangað til landa sem þú vilt.	"Then give I to-you free-wealth and travel you shopping-travelling there to lands as you wish".	"Then I give to you free wealth and you may travel and purchase there lands as you wish".
Hann lést eigi það vildu.	He had not that willed.	He said that he did not wish for this.
Þá mælti konungur:	Then said the-king:	Then the king said:
"Vandast mér nú heldur því að eftir hefi eg nú leitað sem eg kann.	"Difficult for-me now rather because that after have I now sought that-which I can	"This is rather difficult for me now after I have sought all that I can.
Og er nú einn eftir hluturinn og er sá alllítils verður hjá þessum er eg hefi boðið þér en þó kann eigi geta hvað helst hlýðir.	And is it now one after thing and is so little worth next-to these that I have offered to-you but though know not get what preferably obeys".	And now there is one thing after that is of little worth next to these that I have offered to you, but though one can not know what is best".
"Far þú nú hvern dag þá er borð eru uppi á fund minn og eg sit eigi um nauðsynjamálum og mun eg hjala við þig.	"Travel you now each day then to tables they-are up to find mine and I sit not about needful-matters and shall I talk with you	"You shall travel each day then to my tables when they are up to find me, when I am not sitting on needful matters, and I shall talk with you.
Skulum við ræða um konu þessa alla vega þess er þú vilt og má í hug koma og mun eg gefa mér tóm til þessa því að það verður stundum að mönnum verður harms síns að léttara er um er rætt.	We-shall with discuss about woman this all ways this that you wish and may to thought come and shall I give myself time to this accordingly that it becomes awhile that men becomes sorrow theirs that lightened are about is discussed.	We-shall with discuss about this woman all ways that you wish and may come to mind, and shall I give myself time to this accordingly, that it becomes after a while that men's sorrow becomes lightened when it is talked about.
Og það skal og þessu fylgja að aldrei skaltu gjaflaust í brott fara frá mínum fundi.	And that shall and this follow that never shall-you gitfless to away travel from my meeting".	And this shall follow, that you shall never travel away from my meeting without a gift".
Ívar svaraði:	Ivar answered:	Ivar answered:
"Þetta vil eg herra og haf þökk fyrir eftirleituna.	"That will I lord and have thanks for after-seeking".	"That I wish for lord, and I have thanks for your consideration".

The Tale of Ívarr Son of Ingimundr (Old Icelandic)

Old Icelandic	Literal	English
Og nú gera þeir svo að jafnan er konungur situr eigi yfir vandamálum þá talar hann oft um þessa konu við Ívar.	And now did they so to equally and the-king sat not over problems then talk he often about this woman with Ivar.	And now they did so, equally the king sat over problems, and then talked often about this woman with Ivar.
Og þetta hlýddi bragðið og bættist nú Ívari harms síns vonum bráðara.	And this followed looked and improved now Ivar's grief his hoped sooner-than.	And so it followed, that it looked that now to Ivar that his grief improved sonner than he had hoped.
Gladdist hann eftir þetta og kemur í samt lag sem fyrr hafði verið um skemmtun hans og gleði.	Gladdest he after this and came to same place as before had been about amusement his and gladness.	Gladdened was he after this, and it came to the same as it was before, his amusement and gladness.
Og er hann með Eysteini.	And was he with Eystein.	And he remained with Eystein.

Word List (Old Icelandic to English)

Old Icelandic	English

A, a

að	by, from, of, that, to
af	of, off
aftur	back
aldrei	never
alla	all
alllítils	little
allra	of-all
annar	another

Á, á

á	has, that, to
áður	before
ástmenn	beloved-friends
ástsamlega	affectionate

Æ, æ

æ	ever
ætt	ancestry

B, b

bað	ask
bættist	improved
bauð	offered
bera	carry
biði	wait-for
bjóst	prepare
boðið	offered
borð	tables
bráðara	sooner-than
bræður	brothers
bragðið	looked
bréf	letters
bróðir	brother
bróður	brother
brott	away

D, d

dag	day
draga	drag
dýrðarmaður	glorious-man

E, e

eða	and, or
ef	if
eftir	after
eftirleituna	after-seeking
eftirsjá	look-back
eg	I
eiga	posess
eigi	none, not, owns
eignum	owning
eigur	ownership
einhverja	one
einn	one
ekki	not
en	but, that
engi	no
er	and, are, as, has, if, is, is it, it-is, that, to, was, when, who
ertu	you-are
eru	are, are-there, is-there, they-are
Eysteini	Eystein (name)
Eysteinn	Eystein (name)
Eysteins	Eystein (name)

F, f

fá	get, give
fæ	give
fagrar	fair
fann	found

Word List (Old Icelandic to English)

Old Icelandic	English	Old Icelandic	English
far	travel	hans	he, him, his
fara	travel	harmi	grief
farið	going	harms	grief, sorrow
fé	wealth	harmur	grief
fékk	married	hefi	have
fer	travelled	hefir	have
ferð	travel	heimti	summoned
fór	travelled	heldur	rather
forræði	authority, power	helst	preferably
frá	from, of	hennar	her
framar	from	hér	here
fund	find, meet	herra	lord
fundi	meeting	hét	named, was-named
fundist	found	hjá	next-to
fylgja	follow	hjala	talk
fyrir	for	hlut	matter, part
fyrr	before	hluti	things
		hluturinn	thing
		hlýddi	followed
		hlýðir	obeys
		höfum	have

G, g

Old Icelandic	English	Old Icelandic	English
gefa	give	honum	he, him
gera	did	hug	thought
gert	done	hugkvæmur	thoughtful
geta	get, guess	hugsjúkur	mind-sick
getan	guessing	hún	she
getist	estimate	hvað	that, what
gifta	give-in-marriage	hve	how
giftist	be-married	hver	who
gjaflaust	gitfless	hverfum	let-us-go
gladdist	gladdest	hvern	each
gleði	gladness	hví	why
góðu	good		
gott	good		
grun	suspicion		

I, i

Old Icelandic	English
illa	bad
Ingimundarson	son-of-Ingimundur (name)
innsigli	royal-seal

H, h

Old Icelandic	English
haf	have
hafa	have, having, to-have
hafði	had
haft	had
hana	her
handa	hand
hann	he, he-was, him

Í, í

Old Icelandic	English
í	in, to
Íslands	Iceland (place)

Word List (Old Icelandic to English)

Old Icelandic	English
íslenskur	Icelander
Ívar	Ivar (name)
Ívari	Ivar's (name)
Ívars	Ivar's (name)

J, j

Old Icelandic	English
jafnan	equally
jafnmenni	equal-to
Jóansdóttur	Joansdottir (name)
jólin	Yule

K, k

Old Icelandic	English
kann	can, know
kaupferðir	shopping-travelling
kemur	came
kom	came
koma	come
komið	become
konar	kinds-of
konu	woman
konuna	a-wife, this-woman
konungbornar	kings-born
konungi	the-king
konungs	the-king
konungur	king, the-king
konur	woman, women
kurteisar	polite
kveður	said
kvenna	women
kyni	kin

L, l

Old Icelandic	English
lag	place
landa	lands
landi	land
landinu	the-land
lausafé	free-wealth
leita	asking, seek
leitað	sought
lést	had
lét	had
léttara	lightened
litlu	a-little

M, m

Old Icelandic	English
má	may, may-be
maður	man
mæla	say
mælti	said
máli	matter
málinu	the-matter
máls	speak
manna	men, people's
margar	many
margs	many
marka	marked
með	with
meiri	greater
menn	man
mér	for-me, me, myself, to-me
mest	the-most
mig	mine
mikið	greatly, much
mikils	much
mikla	much
minn	mine, my
minna	less
minnir	memory
mínu	my
mínum	my
mitt	mine
mjög	much
mönnum	men
mörgum	many
mun	shall, should
muntu	shall, should-you

N, n

Old Icelandic	English
ná	get
nauðsynjamálum	needful-matters
naut	enjoyed

Word List (Old Icelandic to English)

Old Icelandic	English
neitti	nothing
njóta	enjoy
nokkur	any, some
nokkura	any
nokkurar	some
nokkurir	some
nokkurum	anything
nú	now

O, o

Old Icelandic	English
Oddnýjar	Oddny (name)
Oddnýju	Oddynja (name)
oft	often
og	and
orð	word
orðum	words
oss	ours, us

Ó, ó

Old Icelandic	English
ógleði	sadness
ógnarorðum	menacing-words
ókátur	displeased

Ö, ö

Old Icelandic	English
öngu	none

R, r

Old Icelandic	English
ráð	advise, decision
ráða	power
ræða	discuss
rætt	discussed
reiðfari	travelled

S, s

Old Icelandic	English
sá	so, that
samt	same
sé	say, see, yourself
séð	seen
seg	say
segir	said
segja	say
sem	as, that-which, which
sér	he, her
síðan	afterwards, then
síðar	later
sig	him
sína	his
síns	his, theirs
sit	sit
situr	sat
sjá	see
skal	shall
skáld	poet
skaltu	shall-you
skemmtan	amusement
skemmtir	amuse
skemmtun	amusement
skildust	parted
skulum	we-shall
skyldi	should
sóma	honour
spurði	asked
stórættaður	large-family
stundum	awhile
svaraði	answered
svo	so, such
sýnist	seems

T, t

Old Icelandic	English
talar	talk
tekur	took
til	to
tók	took
tóm	time

Þ, þ

Old Icelandic	English
þá	then
það	it, that, the

Word List (Old Icelandic to English)

Old Icelandic	English
þær	therefore
þangað	there
þar	here, there, there, therefore
þau	then
þegar	as-soon
þeim	theirs
þeima	that
þeir	they
þeirra	they, those
þér	to-you, you, yourself
þess	this
þessa	this
þessar	this
þessu	this
þessum	these, this
þetta	that, this
þig	you
þó	nevertheless, though, yet
þökk	thanks
Þorfinnur	Thorfin (name), Thorfin (name)
þótti	thought, thought
þú	to-you, you
þunglegar	difficult, the-heavier
þurfa	needed
því	accordingly, because, since, such, that, therefore
þykist	seeming
þykja	be-valued

U, u

um	about, about-it
undi	part
uni	like
unir	satisfied
uppi	up
utan	out

Ú, ú

úr	of
út	out

V, v

væri	was
vandamálum	problems
vandast	difficult
var	was, were
varð	was
veg	way
vega	ways
veislur	feasts
veit	know
vel	well
ver	be
vér	we
vera	be, being, was
verður	becomes, worth
verið	been
við	with
víkja	give-in
vil	will, wish
vildir	wish
vildu	willed
vilt	wish
viltu	will-you
vinhollur	friend-whole
vinmælum	friendly-words
virti	worthed
viti	knew
vitur	wise
vonir	hopes
vonum	hoped
vorar	spring
voruð	were
vorum	our

Y, y

yðru	your
yðrum	your
yfir	over
yfirlæti	favour

Word List (English to Old Icelandic)

English	Old Icelandic
A, a	
about	um
about-it	um
accordingly	því
advise	ráð
affectionate	ástsamlega
after	eftir
after-seeking	eftirleituna
afterwards	síðan
a-little	litlu
all	alla
amuse	skemmtir
amusement	skemmtan, skemmtun
ancestry	ætt
and	eða, er, og
another	annar
answered	svaraði
any	nokkur, nokkura
anything	nokkurum
are	er, eru
are-there	eru
as	er, sem
ask	bað
asked	spurði
asking	leita
as-soon	þegar
authority	forræði
away	brott
awhile	stundum
a-wife	konuna
B, b	
back	aftur
bad	illa
be	ver, vera
because	því
become	komið
becomes	verður
been	verið
before	áður, fyrr
being	vera
beloved-friends	ástmenn
be-married	giftist
be-valued	þykja
brother	bróðir, bróður
brothers	bræður
but	en
by	að
C, c	
came	kemur, kom
can	kann
carry	bera
come	koma
D, d	
day	dag
decision	ráð
did	gera
difficult	þunglegar, vandast
discuss	ræða
discussed	rætt
displeased	ókátur
done	gert
drag	draga
E, e	
each	hvern
enjoy	njóta
enjoyed	naut
equally	jafnan
equal-to	jafnmenni
estimate	getist
ever	æ
Eystein (name)	Eysteini, Eysteinn, Eysteins

Word List (English to Old Icelandic)

English	Old Icelandic

F, f

fair	fagrar
favour	yfirlæti
feasts	veislur
find	fund
follow	fylgja
followed	hlýddi
for	fyrir
for-me	mér
found	fann, fundist
free-wealth	lausafé
friendly-words	vinmælum
friend-whole	vinhollur
from	að, frá, framar

G, g

get	fá, geta, ná
gitfless	gjaflaust
give	fá, fæ, gefa
give-in	víkja
give-in-marriage	gifta
gladdest	gladdist
gladness	gleði
glorious-man	dýrðarmaður
going	farið
good	góðu, gott
greater	meiri
greatly	mikið
grief	harmi, harms, harmur
guess	geta
guessing	getan

H, h

had	hafði, haft, lést, lét
hand	handa
has	á, er
have	haf, hafa, hefi, hefir, höfum
having	hafa

English	Old Icelandic
he	hann, hans, honum, sér
her	hana, hennar, sér
here	hér, þar
he-was	hann
him	hann, hans, honum, sig
his	hans, sína, síns
honour	sóma
hoped	vonum
hopes	vonir
how	hve

I, i

I	eg
Iceland (place)	Íslands
Icelander	íslenskur
if	ef, er
improved	bættist
in	í
is	er
is it	er
is-there	eru
it	það
it-is	er
Ivar (name)	Ívar
Ivar's (name)	Ívari, Ívars

J, j

Joansdottir (name)	Jóansdóttur

K, k

kin	kyni
kinds-of	konar
king	konungur
kings-born	konungbornar
knew	viti
know	kann, veit

Word List (English to Old Icelandic)

English	Old Icelandic

L, l

land	landi
lands	landa
large-family	stórættaður
later	síðar
less	minna
letters	bréf
let-us-go	hverfum
lightened	léttara
like	uni
little	alllítils
look-back	eftirsjá
looked	bragðið
lord	herra

M, m

man	maður, menn
many	margar, margs, mörgum
marked	marka
married	fékk
matter	hlut, máli
may	má
may-be	má
me	mér
meet	fund
meeting	fundi
memory	minnir
men	manna, mönnum
menacing-words	ógnarorðum
mind-sick	hugsjúkur
mine	mig, minn, mitt
much	mikið, mikils, mikla, mjög
my	minn, mínu, mínum
myself	mér

N, n

named	hét
needed	þurfa
needful-matters	nauðsynjamálum
never	aldrei
nevertheless	þó
next-to	hjá
no	engi
none	eigi, öngu
not	eigi, ekki
nothing	neitti
now	nú

O, o

obeys	hlýðir
Oddny (name)	Oddnýjar
Oddynja (name)	Oddnýju
of	að, af, frá, úr
of-all	allra
off	af
offered	bauð, boðið
often	oft
one	einhverja, einn
or	eða
our	vorum
ours	oss
out	út, utan
over	yfir
ownership	eigur
owning	eignum
owns	eigi

P, p

part	hlut, undi
parted	skildust
people's	manna
place	lag
poet	skáld
polite	kurteisar
posess	eiga
power	forræði, ráða
preferably	helst
prepare	bjóst
problems	vandamálum

Word List (English to Old Icelandic)

English	Old Icelandic

R, r

English	Old Icelandic
rather	heldur
royal-seal	innsigli

S, s

English	Old Icelandic
sadness	ógleði
said	kveður, mælti, segir
same	samt
sat	situr
satisfied	unir
say	mæla, sé, seg, segja
see	sé, sjá
seek	leita
seeming	þykist
seems	sýnist
seen	séð
shall	mun, muntu, skal
shall-you	skaltu
she	hún
shopping-travelling	kaupferðir
should	mun, skyldi
should-you	muntu
since	því
sit	sit
so	sá, svo
some	nokkur, nokkurar, nokkurir
son-of-Ingimundur (name)	Ingimundarson
sooner-than	bráðara
sorrow	harms
sought	leitað
speak	máls
spring	vorar
such	svo, því
summoned	heimti
suspicion	grun

T, t

English	Old Icelandic
tables	borð
talk	hjala, talar
thanks	þökk
that	á, að, en, er, hvað, sá, það, þeima, þetta, því
that-which	sem
the	það
the-heavier	þunglegar
theirs	síns, þeim
the-king	konungi, konungs, konungur
the-land	landinu
the-matter	málinu
the-most	mest
then	síðan, þá, þau
there	þangað, þar
therefore	þær, þar, því
these	þessum
they	þeir, þeirra
they-are	eru
thing	hluturinn
things	hluti
this	þess, þessa, þessar, þessu, þessum, þetta
this-woman	konuna
Thorfin (name)	Þorfinnur
those	þeirra
though	þó
thought	hug, þótti
thoughtful	hugkvæmur
time	tóm
to	á, að, er, í, til
to-have	hafa
to-me	mér
took	tekur, tók
to-you	þér, þú
travel	far, fara, ferð
travelled	fer, fór, reiðfari

U, u

English	Old Icelandic
up	uppi
us	oss

Word List (English to Old Icelandic)

English	Old Icelandic

W, w

wait-for	biði
was	er, væri, var, varð, vera
was-named	hét
way	veg
ways	vega
we	vér
wealth	fé
well	vel
were	var, voruð
we-shall	skulum
what	hvað
when	er
which	sem
who	er, hver
why	hví
will	vil
willed	vildu
will-you	viltu
wise	vitur
wish	vil, vildir, vilt
with	með, við
woman	konu, konur
women	konur, kvenna
word	orð
words	orðum
worth	verður
worthed	virti

Y, y

yet	þó
you	þér, þig, þú
you-are	ertu
your	yðru, yðrum
yourself	sé, þér
Yule	jólin

A Word Comparison of Old Norse and Old Icelandic Words

Old Norse	Old Icelandic	English
áðr	áður	before
aftr	aftur	back
aldri	aldrei	never
annarr	annar	another
ástsamliga	ástsamlega	affectionate
at	að	by
at	að	from
at	að	of
at	að	that
at	að	to
boðit	boðið	offered
bræðr	bræður	brothers
bragðit	bragðið	looked
dýrðarmaðr	dýrðarmaður	glorious-man
eftirleitunina	eftirleituna	after-seeking
eigu	eiga	posess
ek	eg	I
engu	öngu	none
farit	farið	going
fekk	fékk	married
ferr	fer	travelled
ferr	ferð	travel
fundizt	fundist	found
harmr	harmur	grief
heimtí	heimti	summoned
heldr	heldur	rather
helzt	helst	preferably
hlutrinn	hluturinn	thing
hon	hún	she
hugkvæmr	hugkvæmur	thoughtful
hugsjúkr	hugsjúkur	mind-sick
hvat	hvað	that
hvat	hvað	what
hverr	hver	who
íslenzkr	íslenskur	Icelander
Ívarr	Ívar	Ivar (name)
kemr	kemur	came
komit	komið	become
konungr	konungur	king
konungr	konungur	the-king
kveðr	kveður	said
leitat	leitað	sought
lézt	lést	had
maðr	maður	man
mik	mig	mine
mikit	mikið	greatly
mikit	mikið	much
minum	mínum	my
mjök	mjög	much
nökkur	nokkur	any
nökkur	nokkur	some
nökkura	nokkura	any
nökkurar	nokkurar	some
nökkurir	nokkurir	some
nökkurum	nokkurum	anything
ok	og	and
ókátr	ókátur	displeased
ór	úr	of
sét	séð	seen
sik	sig	him
sitk	sit	sit
sitr	situr	sat
skilðist	skildust	parted
stórættaðr	stórættaður	large-family
svá	svo	so
svá	svo	such
tekr	tekur	took
þangat	þangað	there
þat	það	it
þat	það	that
þat	það	the
þeira	þeirra	they
þeira	þeirra	those
þik	þig	you
Þorfiðr	Þorfinnur	Thorfin (name)
Þorfinnr	Þorfinnur	Thorfin (name)

A Word Comparison of Old Norse and Old Icelandic

Old Norse	Old Icelandic	English
þungligar	þunglegar	difficult
þungligar	þunglegar	the-heavier
þykkist	þykist	seeming
þykkja	þykja	be-valued
unði	undi	part
útan	utan	out
vánir	vonir	hopes
vánum	vonum	hoped
várar	vorar	spring
váruð	voruð	were
várum	vorum	our
veizlur	veislur	feasts
verðr	verður	becomes
verðr	verður	worth
verit	verið	been
vill	vilt	wish
villtu	viltu	will-you
vinhollr	vinhollur	friend-whole
virði	virti	worthed
vit	við	with
vita	viti	knew
vitr	vitur	wise

www.ingramcontent.com/pod-product-compliance
Lightning Source LLC
Chambersburg PA
CBHW051427070526
44584CB00023B/3612